Mary Hoffman has written more than 80 books for children and in 1998 was made an Honorary Fellow of the Library Association for services to children and libraries. She is also the editor of a quarterly children's online book review called *Armadillo*. In 1992 *Amazing Grace*, her first book for Frances Lincoln, was selected for Children's Book of the Year and commended for the Kate Greenaway Medal. It was followed by *Grace & family, An Angel Just Like Me, A Twist in the Tail, Women of Camelot, Seven Wonders of the Ancient World*, and three Grace storybooks *Starring Grace, Encore, Grace!* and *Bravo, Grace!*

Caroline Binch has illustrated children's books for Rosa Guy, Oralee Wachter and Grace Nichols as well as writing and illustrating a number of her own titles. Her illustrations for Rita Phillips Mitchell's *Hue Boy* and *Down by the River* were shortlisted for the Kate Greenaway Medal in 1993 and 1996, with *Hue Boy* going on to win the Smarties Prize. Caroline is perhaps best known for illustrating Mary Hoffman's bestselling picture books *Amazing Grace*, which was shortlisted for the Kate Greenaway Medal, and *Grace & family*, and the storybook *Starring Grace*, all published by Frances Lincoln. Her other Frances Lincoln titles are *Since Dad Left*, winner of the United Kingdom Book Award in 1998, *Silver Shoes*, shortlisted for the Kate Greenaway Medal in 2002, and *Petar's Song*, written by Pratima Mitchell.

For Sue Lubeck, who couldn't wait – M.H.

For Taj and all the Mahals:
"*Families are what you make them.*" – C.B.

Grace & family copyright © Frances Lincoln Limited 1995
Text copyright © Mary Hoffman 1995
Illustrations copyright © Caroline Binch 1995

First published in Great Britain in 1995 by
Frances Lincoln Children's Books, 4 Torriano Mews,
Torriano Avenue, London NW5 2RZ
www.franceslincoln.com

This paperback edition published in 2007

All rights reserved

No part of this publication may be reproduced, stored in a retrieval system, or transmitted,
in any form, or by any means, electrical, mechanical, photocopying, recording or otherwise
without the prior written permission of the publisher or a licence permitting restricted copying.
In the United Kingdom such licences are issued by the Copyright Licensing Agency,
Saffron House, 6-10 Kirby Street, London EC1N 8TS.

British Library Cataloguing in Publication Data available on request

ISBN 978-1-84507-750-1

Printed in China

1 3 5 7 9 8 6 4 2

Grace & family

Mary Hoffman
Illustrated by
Caroline Binch

F
FRANCES LINCOLN
CHILDREN'S BOOKS

Grace lived with her Ma and her Nana and a cat called Paw-Paw. Next to her family, what Grace liked best was stories. Some she knew and some she made up, and she was particularly interested in ones about fathers, because she didn't have one.

"You do too have a father," her Ma said when she caught Grace talking that way. "I must have told you a hundred times about how we split up and your Papa went back to Africa. He has another family now, but he's still your father, even though he doesn't live with us any more."

Well, that wasn't Grace's idea of a father! She wanted one like Beauty's, who brought her roses from the Beast's garden in spite of the dangers. Not one she hadn't seen since she was very little and only knew from letters and photographs.

And in her school reading books Grace saw that all the families had a mother and a father, a boy and a girl, and a dog and a cat.

"Our family's not right," she told Nana. "We need a father and a brother and a dog."

"Well," said Nana, "I'm not sure how Paw-Paw would feel about a dog. And what about me? Are there any Nanas in your school book?"

Grace shook her head.

"So do you want me to go?" asked Nana, smiling.

"Of course not!" Grace said, hugging her. Nana hugged her back.

"Families are what you make them," she said.

Then, one day when Grace got in from school she saw a letter on the table with a crocodile stamp on it. Grace knew it must be from Papa, but it wasn't Christmas or her birthday.

Ma said, "Guess what! Your Papa sent the money for two tickets to visit him in Africa for the Easter holidays. Nana says she'll go with you if you want. What do you say?"

But Grace was speechless. She had made up so many fathers for herself she had forgotten what the real one was like.

Grace and Nana left for Africa on a very cold grey day. They arrived in The Gambia in golden sunshine like the hottest summer back home. It had been a long, long journey. Grace barely noticed the strange sights and sounds that greeted her. She was thinking of Papa.

"I wonder if he will still love me?" thought Grace. "He has other children now and in stories it's always the youngest that is the favourite." She held on tightly to Nana.

Outside the airport was a man who looked a little like Papa's photo. He swung Grace up in his arms and held her close. Grace buried her nose in his shirt and thought, "I do remember."

In the car she started to notice how different everything seemed. There were sheep wandering along the roadside and people selling watermelons under the trees.

And when they reached her father's compound, there was the biggest difference of all. A pretty young woman with a little girl and a baby boy came to meet them. Grace said hello but couldn't manage another word all evening. Everyone thought she was just tired. Except Nana.

"What's the matter, honey?" she asked when they went to bed. "You've got a father and a brother now and they even have a dog!"

But Grace thought, "They make a storybook family without me. I'm one girl too many. Besides, it's the wrong Ma."

The next day, Grace started to get to know Neneh and Bakary. The children thought it was wonderful to have a big sister all the way from England. And Grace couldn't help liking them too. But she had to feel cross with someone.

Grace knew lots of stories about wicked stepmothers – Cinderella, Snow White, Hansel and Gretel – so she decided to be cross with Jatou. "I won't clean the house for her," thought Grace, "I won't eat anything she cooks and I won't let her take me into the forest."

Jatou made a big dish of savoury benachim for lunch, but Grace wouldn't eat any. "I'm not hungry," she said.

"She's probably still getting over the long flight," said Jatou.

When Papa came home from work, he found Grace in the backyard. He sat beside her under the big old jackfruit tree.

"This is where my grandma used to tell me stories when I was a little boy," he said.

"Nana tells me stories too," said Grace.

"Did she ever tell you the one about how your Ma and I came to split up?" asked Papa.

"I know that one," said Grace, "but I don't want to hear it right now," and she covered up her ears.

Papa hugged her. "Would you like the one about the Papa who loved his little girl so much he saved up all his money to bring her to visit him?"

"Yes, I'd like that one," said Grace.

"OK. But if I tell you that story, will you promise me to try to be nice to Jatou? You're both very important to me," said Papa.

Grace thought about it. "I'll try," she said.

Next day, they went to the food market. It was much more exciting than shopping at home. Even the money had crocodiles on it! Lots of the women carried their shopping on their heads.

Then they went to a stall which was like stepping inside a rainbow. There was cloth with crocodiles and elephants on it and cloth with patterns made from pebbles and shells. And so many colours!

"We can choose cloth for Grace's first African dress," said Papa. Grace and Nana spent a long time choosing. No one was in a hurry.

The days of Grace's visit flew by. She played in the ocean with her brother and sister, and she told them a bedtime story every night. She told all the stories she knew – Beauty and the Beast, Rapunzel, Rumpelstiltskin. It was amazing how many stories were about fathers who gave their daughters away. But she didn't tell them any about wicked stepmothers.

Sometimes Ma rang up from home, and then Grace felt strange. "I feel like gum stretched out all thin in a bubble," she told Nana. "As if there isn't enough of me to go round. I can't manage two families. What if I burst?"

"Families are what you make them," said Nana. "A family with you in it is your family."

Soon it was their last evening and there was a big farewell party at the compound. Grace and Nana wore their African clothes and Grace ate twice as much benachim as everyone else.

"Now you really might burst," said Nana.

But Grace wasn't worried about bursting any more.
She just wanted to dance with her African family.

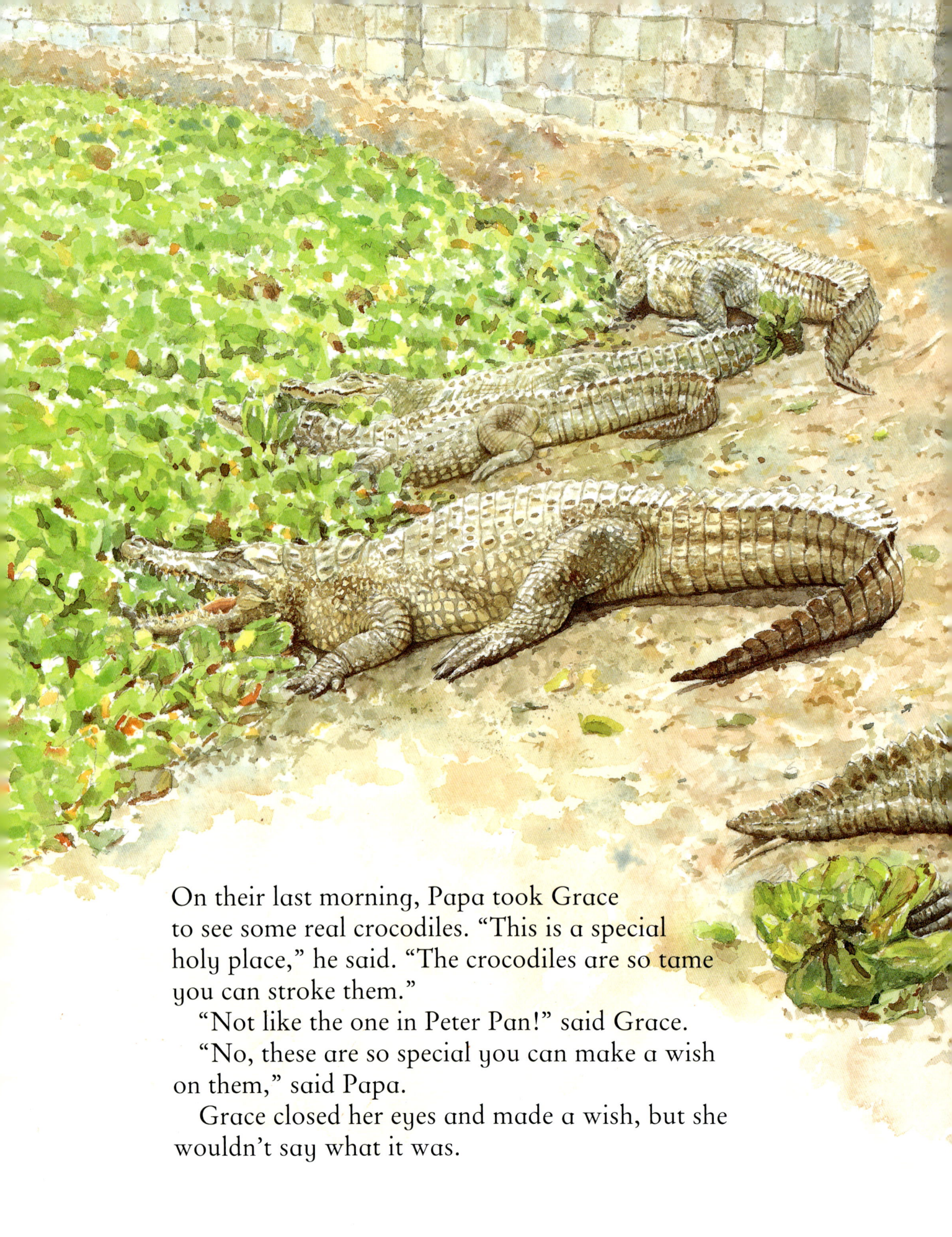

On their last morning, Papa took Grace to see some real crocodiles. "This is a special holy place," he said. "The crocodiles are so tame you can stroke them."

"Not like the one in Peter Pan!" said Grace.

"No, these are so special you can make a wish on them," said Papa.

Grace closed her eyes and made a wish, but she wouldn't say what it was.

Later at the compound, Grace asked Nana, "Why aren't there any stories about families like mine, that don't live together?"

"Well at least you've stopped thinking it's your family that's wrong," said Nana. "Now all you have to do is make up a new story to go with it."

"I'll do that," said Grace, "and when we're home again, I'll write it down and send it to Jatou to read to Neneh and Bakary."

The whole family came to see them off at the airport. Grace was sorry to say goodbye to her stepmother and her new brother and sister. But leaving Papa was hardest of all.

Waiting for their plane, Nana asked Grace if she had thought any more about her story.

"Yes, but I can't think of the right ending," said Grace, "because the story's still going on."

"How about they lived happily ever after?" asked Nana.

"That's a good one," said Grace. "Or they lived happily ever after, though not all in the same place."

"Stories are what you make them," said Nana.

"Just like families," said Grace.

MORE TITLES FROM FRANCES LINCOLN CHILDREN'S BOOKS

Amazing Grace
Mary Hoffman
Illustrated by Caroline Binch

Grace loves to act out stories. Sometimes she plays the leading part, sometimes she is a cast of thousands. At Christmas time, when her school decides to perform *Peter Pan*, Grace longs to play Peter, but her classmates say that Peter was a boy and besides, he wasn't black… But with the support of her mother and grandmother, Grace soon discovers that if you set your mind to it, you can do anything you want to.

ISBN 978-0-7112-0699-1

Gregory Cool
Caroline Binch

When a cool city boy meets the full warmth of the Caribbean, anything can happen. Gregory is determined not to enjoy himself when he is sent off to visit his grandparents in rural Tobago. After a whole variety of adventures, however, he begins to think that life outside the city may not be so bad after all.

ISBN 978-0-7112-0890-2

Starring Grace
Mary Hoffman

Grace the Explorer, Grace the Detective, Grace the Astronaut…
In this lively collection of eight stories Grace embarks on a new series of dramatic holiday adventures with her friends, using her imagination to become just about anything she wants!

ISBN 978-0-7112-2140-6

Frances Lincoln titles are available from all good bookshops.
You can also buy books and find out more about your favourite titles, authors and illustrators on our website: www.franceslincoln.com